ANCIENT FORESTS

W9-BXZ-336

Discovering Nature

By
Margaret Anderson
Nancy Field
Karen Stephenson

Illustrated by Sharon Torvik

ISBN 0-941042-14-6

 Printed on Recycled Paper with Soy Ink

Exploring an Ancient Forest . . .

is like a journey to another time. The giant trees are part of history. Their scars and growth rings hold clues to fires, drought, and storms that happened long ago.

Imagine yourself standing in a patch of filtered sunlight deep inside an ancient forest. Above you, the swaying treetops seem to touch the sky. You point your camera straight up and take a picture. Now you kneel down and snap a close-up of a small pink flower. The ground is soft and springy. Everywhere you look, you see different shades of green – green moss, green leaves, green pine needles. Lichens hang from branches like pale green beards.

The silence is broken by a woodpecker tapping out a rhythm as it searches for its dinner. A branch creaks. With luck you may hear the voice of a rare giant salamander. It barks like a small dog. The gurgling sound of running water tells you there's a stream close by.

The way to the stream is blocked by a fallen log so big you can't see over it. You scramble onto a smaller log and boost yourself up. Mountain blueberry bushes are growing on top of the log! You sample a few berries. How can bushes grow on a dead tree? On the other side of the log you spot a bright yellow slime mold. It will make a colorful picture.

When you reach the stream another fallen tree provides a handy bridge. When did all those trees fall? How old were they when they fell? By now your mind is full of questions about the ancient forest. You'll find some of the answers by doing the activities in this book.

What is an ancient forest?
See pages 4 to 7

Where can I find ancient forests?
See pages 15 to 18

What is a nurse log?
See page 8

How can a small mammal help a tree grow? *See pages 24 and 25*

Who lives in the forest?
See pages 5, 8 to 11

How do ancient forests affect the ocean? *See page 26*

Why are spotted owls
having a hard time?
Play the game on pages 29 to 31

What can I do to
save ancient forests?
See page 36

A Living Giant

Five hundred years ago fire swept up a steep mountainside. A tiny seed landed on the burned ground. The seed sprouted, pushing soft green needles out of the blackened earth.

A hundred years later, it had grown into a tall Douglas-fir tree. Of course, it wasn't called a Douglas-fir back then. David Douglas, the botanist and explorer who gave the tree its name, wouldn't be born for another two centuries.

The tree continued to grow, reaching up towards the sky. And it is growing still. It is now 250 feet (76.2 m) tall and measures 45 feet (13.7 m) around the trunk. It has escaped damage from wind, falling trees, and fire. It has also escaped the woodsman's axe and the chainsaw.

Not all the trees in the ancient or **old-growth** forest have been around for as long as this one. Some are newcomers. They got their start when a big tree fell, letting more light reach the forest floor. They may have obtained their nourishment from the rotting wood of the fallen giant.

The different ages, sizes, and kinds of trees in the forest provide many layers for things to live. Some plants and animals find living space and food in the tree tops; some among the lower branches or smaller trees. Still others live among the shrubs or on the forest floor.

How many kids your size, standing on one another's shoulders, would it take to see over a 250-foot Douglas-fir? How many kids would it take to encircle the 45-foot trunk?

Hint: You need to measure the distance from your shoulders to the floor, and the span of your outstretched arms.

The **Douglas squirrel** eats seed cones, dropping piles of scales under the trees.

The **marbled murrelet** is a seabird that nests in the treetops.

The **red tree vole** can spend its whole life in one Douglas-fir tree. It dines on the needles.

The **western red-backed vole** finds its food under ground.

Lichen looks like moss. It grows on the trunks and branches of old trees.

The **Roosevelt elk** eats needles and lichens from branches broken off in winter storms.

5

Forest Neighborhoods

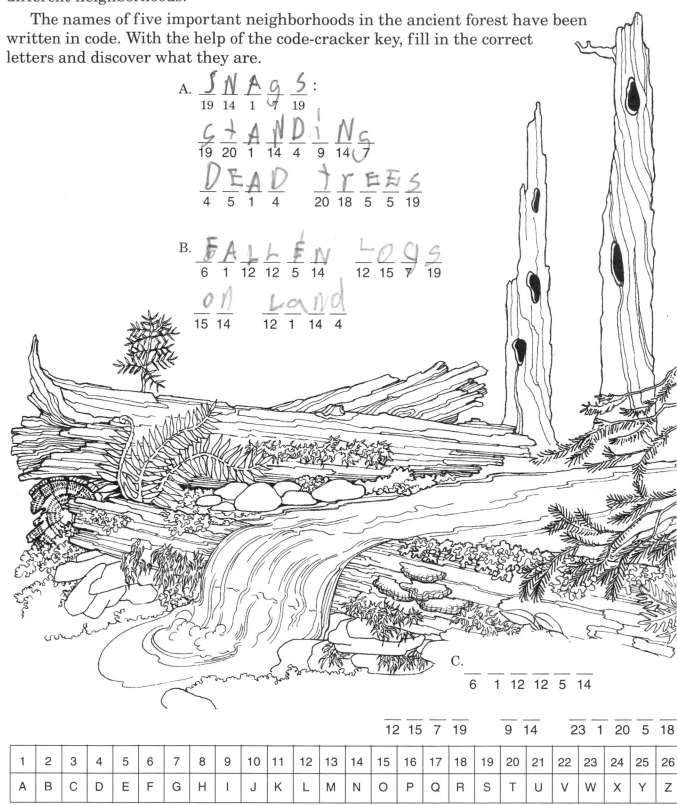

There's more to an ancient forest than trees. Many different kinds of plants and animals make up the forest community. Some cannot live anywhere else. They can all live together in an ancient forest because it offers a wide variety of different neighborhoods.

The names of five important neighborhoods in the ancient forest have been written in code. With the help of the code-cracker key, fill in the correct letters and discover what they are.

A. S N A G S :
   19 14 1 7 19

   S T A N D I N G
   19 20 1 14 4 9 14 7

   D E A D   T R E E S
   4 5 1 4   20 18 5 5 19

B. F A L L E N   L O G S
   6 1 12 12 5 14   12 15 7 19

   O N   L A N D
   15 14   12 1 14 4

C. _ _ _ _ _ _
   6 1 12 12 5 14

   _ _ _ _   _ _   _ _ _ _ _
   12 15 7 19   9 14   23 1 20 5 18

1	2	3	4	5	6	7	8	9	10	11	12	13	14	15	16	17	18	19	20	21	22	23	24	25	26
A	B	C	D	E	F	G	H	I	J	K	L	M	N	O	P	Q	R	S	T	U	V	W	X	Y	Z

D. <u>L a r g E</u>
   12 1 18 7 5

<u>o L D</u>
 15 12 4

<u>t r e e s</u>
 20 18 5 5 19

E. <u>t r e e s</u>   <u>o f</u>   <u>M a n y</u>
  20 18 5 5 19   15 6   13 1 14 25

<u>M a n y</u>   <u>a n D</u>   <u>s i Z e s</u>
 13 1 14 25   1 14 4   19 9 26 5 19

All animals need food, water, and shelter. They need somewhere to hide from enemies and somewhere to raise their young. The place where everything is arranged in a way that makes it possible for the animals to live is called its **habitat**. Plants also need food, water, and a safe place to grow.

Answers on last page

High Density Housing

All sorts of plants and animals are at home around a **fallen log**. The giant salamander rests in the tangled roots. The red-backed vole pauses on the forest floor, hidden by the log from the sharp-eyed hawk. The shy pine marten peers out of its hiding place. The yellow banana slug seeks out the damp shade. The cougar uses the log as a highway through the forest.

The loose bark and crumbling wood provide space for countless other living things. Some of them are too small for us to see. Bacteria produce moisture in decaying wood. A rotting log stays damp even in dry weather. Trapped soil gives ferns and flowers a place to sprout. Sometimes shrubs and trees take root on a log. A log with trees growing on it is called a **nurse log**.

Fallen branches and trees are an important part of the forest. Most were brought down by wind. Heavy snow sometimes breaks branches. Flooded streams can uproot trees. Wind, snow, ice, rain, and even fire are natural forces. They shape the forest by giving new life a chance.

The Recycling Squad

Wood is tough material. That is why we build houses with it. How long it takes to decay depends on the climate, the kind of wood and the activity of the recycling squad. In our homes, termites are pests, but in the forest they do an important job. A fallen tree is a huge food bank. The recycling squad makes this food available to other creatures. This process is called **decomposition**. Insects start the job. A back-up team of mites and fungi soon takes over.

Be a detective. Each of these insects is at home in this rotting log. **Match the numbered clue to the right insect.**

Answers on last page

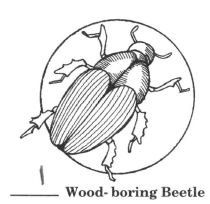

———— **Wood-boring Beetle**

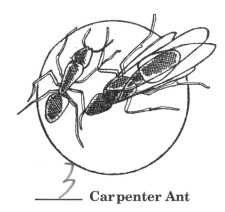

———— **Carpenter Ant**

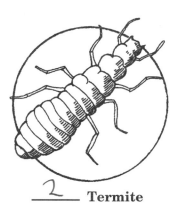

———— **Termite**

A female beetle chews grooves in the inner bark where she lays her eggs. Immature insects, called **larvae**, hatch from the eggs. The larvae go on an eating spree. They chew out new pathways that get wider as the larvae grow.

A queen ant's job is to lay eggs. She lays them in passageways carved out by worker ants with their strong jaws. Workers do not eat wood. They get rid of it by throwing it out through window holes. Other workers bring food in through these openings.

Termites have special bacteria living in their gut that can digest wood. In late summer swarms of winged termites set off to look for a new nest site. After the mating flight, they bite off their wings and start up a new colony in a rotting log.

Apartments and Waterfront Property

 This tall gray **snag** was once a living tree. Even though it is long dead, it is far from lifeless. Creatures make homes in its holes or cavities. Some are into home improvement and dig out bigger holes. Birds perch on its branches. Loose bark provides a hiding place for frogs, bats, beetles and brown creepers. Many animals eat the insects that have burrowed into the wood.

Study the picture and decide where you would find the following: (More than one number can go in a blank.)

_____ Bat shelter

_____ Bobcat home

_____ Hawk perch

_____ Woodpecker food source

_____ Brown creeper nest site

_____ Spotted owl nest site

_____ Flying squirrel den

_____ Beetle homes

_____ Tree frog cover

Over a hundred kinds, or **species**, of animals use snags. When snags are removed, animals find fewer places to live. The habitat is changed and is no longer suitable.

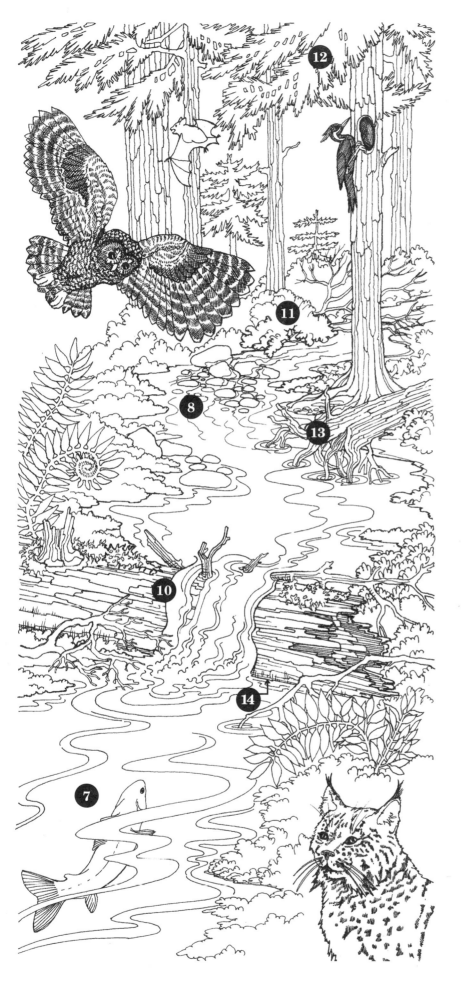

Fallen logs in water change a stream's course. They hold back floating twigs and leaves, turning the water into nutrient soup. They make pools and create rapids that trap bubbles of air. Some animals can only live in oxygen-rich water.

Insects, like stoneflies and caddisflies, find safe footing on submerged bark and branches. They graze the film of algae and bacteria that grows on wet surfaces. Some of these insects become food for fish.

Live trees and shrubs along the bank provide shade. They add twigs, leaves, and berries to the nutrients in the water. Their roots hold the bank in place.

Study the picture and then fill in the blanks. Notice how trees and logs help the stream and its inhabitants. (You may use a number more than once.)

_____ Pools for fish

_____ Shallow water where fish lay eggs

_____ Cover for fish resting and hiding

_____ Bank held in place

_____ Shade helps to keep water cool

_____ Food source for fish

_____ Air bubbles added to water

_____ Food for insects

Answers on last page

An Ancient Forest Mobile

The ancient forest is like a mobile. A mobile is made up of several objects hanging by strings. Each object's weight keeps the entire mobile in balance. Take away one piece and the balance is upset. This is also true in the forest. If one part — such as the dead wood — is removed, the balance is upset.

Plants and animals that share the same environment interact with each other and with the nonliving parts of their surroundings. They form an **ecosystem**. Living and dead trees, ferns, mosses, birds, bugs, fallen leaves, molds, mammals, soil, water, and air are important parts of a forest ecosystem.

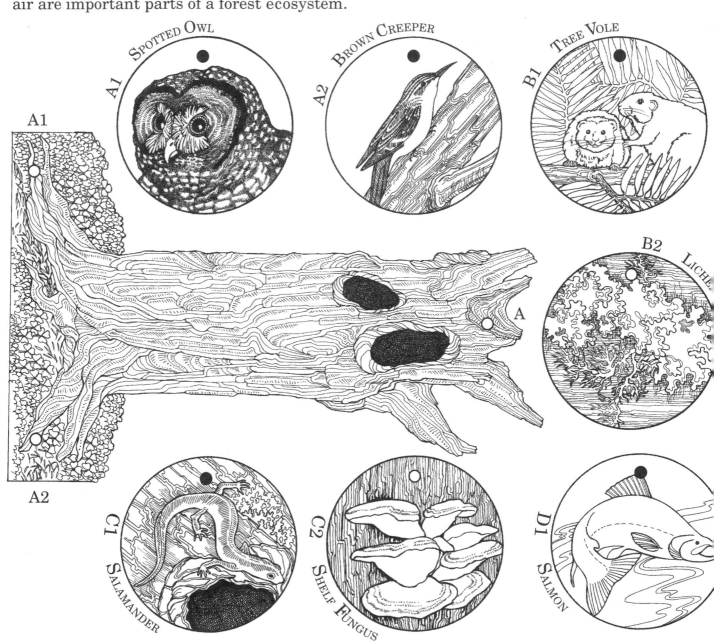

To make your own ancient forest mobile, copy these outlines onto stiff paper and color them. **Matching the letters, assemble your mobile as shown in the diagram on the answer page**. You'll need strong thread, fine string or dental floss and two sticks 12-18 inches long. Tie or pin the sticks in the middle to form a cross.

Copy these patterns. If you cut them out, you won't be able to do the activities on the other side.

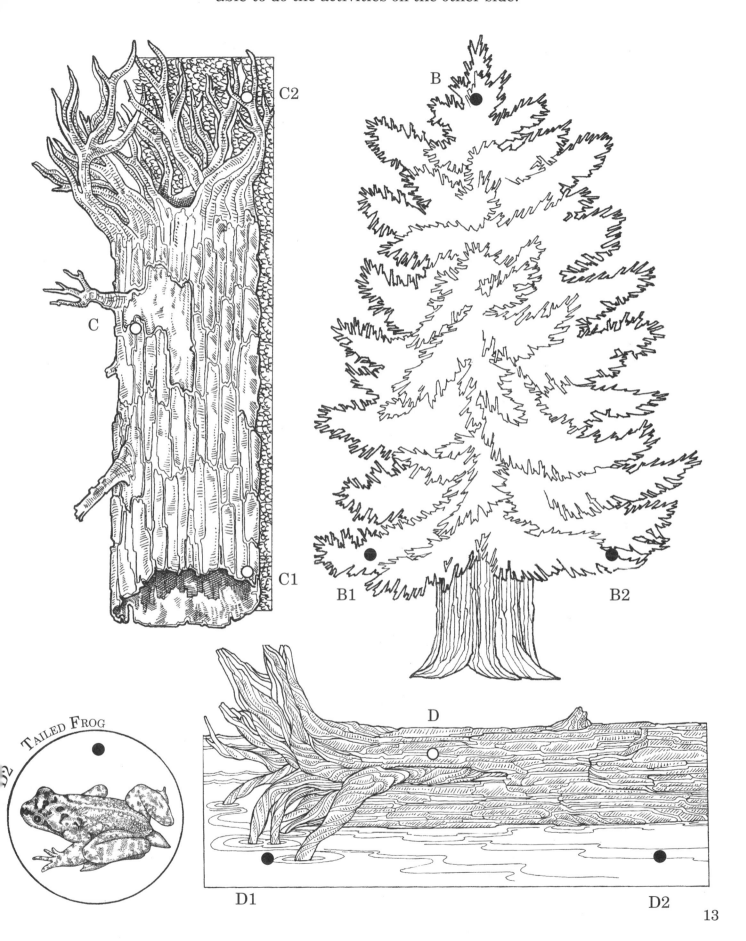

C2

C

C1

B

B1

B2

D

D1

D2

TAILED FROG

D2

Disappearing Forests

In 1620, when the first European settlers came to North America, they found a land covered in forest. They set to work with axes and saws, cutting trees to build houses and to make masts for sailing ships. They cleared the original forest for growing crops. They could not imagine ever running out of trees

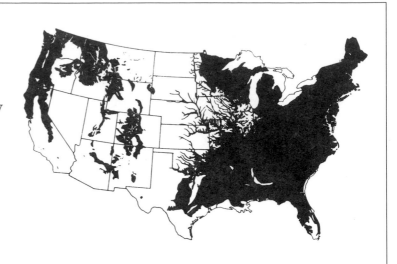

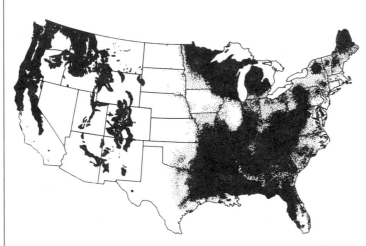

In 1850, large areas of the east had been cleared. However, the westward-bound pioneers had discovered another vast land covered in forest. There were so many big trees that once again they could not imagine ever cutting enough to make a difference. In both Canada and the United States, original forest land was converted to other uses.

In the twentieth century, bulldozers and chainsaws replaced axes and saws. Powerful machines clear mountainsides in a few days. Roads reach farther and farther into the forest. The demand for timber is world wide. It is now easy to see that the ancient forests and the plants and animals that live in them may soon be gone, some of them forever.

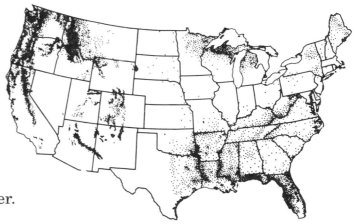

Here are some of the trees and animals you might meet on a Forest Trek across North America. Some of the remaining ancient forests are large. Others are very small.

Sitka spruce is one of the important trees in the forests of Alaska. Sitka spruce is a conifer. The seeds are contained in cones. Conifers have needle-shaped leaves that stay green all year.

Some of the few remaining grizzly bears live in the Douglas-fir and larch forests of the Canadian Rockies. Larch trees are unusual conifers. Their needles turn gold and drop off each fall.

The Haida Indians along the coast of British Columbia carved their great totem poles from cedar. They also used cedar for building houses and canoes, and even used its shredded bark for diapers.

The world's tallest trees are the coastal redwoods of northern California. They live with their heads in the clouds. Fog condenses on the needles and drips down to the forest floor. This fog drip helps them grow.

The spotted owl is an indicator species. It shows the health of the Pacific northwest forests. If these owls nest successfully, other animals that need old-growth forest can also survive.

Awards for the biggest and oldest living things go to trees in the Sierra Nevadas. The biggest sequoia trunk is 40.3 feet (12.3 m) across. A bristlecone pine is the oldest. It grows very slowly. After 4000 years, it is only 30 feet (9.1 m) tall.

Read about more forests on page 18.

Forest Trek

Take a trek across North America and visit patches of ancient forest. Each one is represented by a different symbol. Look for the symbols in the pictures on pages 24 and 27 to learn more about these forests.

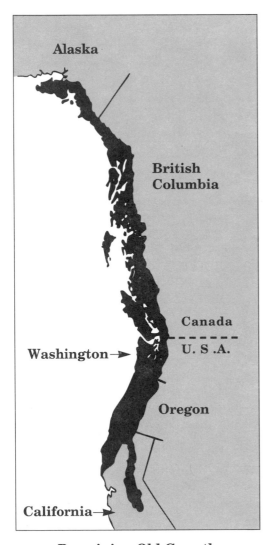

Remaining Old Growth

Most ancient forests in North America have been cut. What remains today is found mainly along the West Coast from Alaska to California.

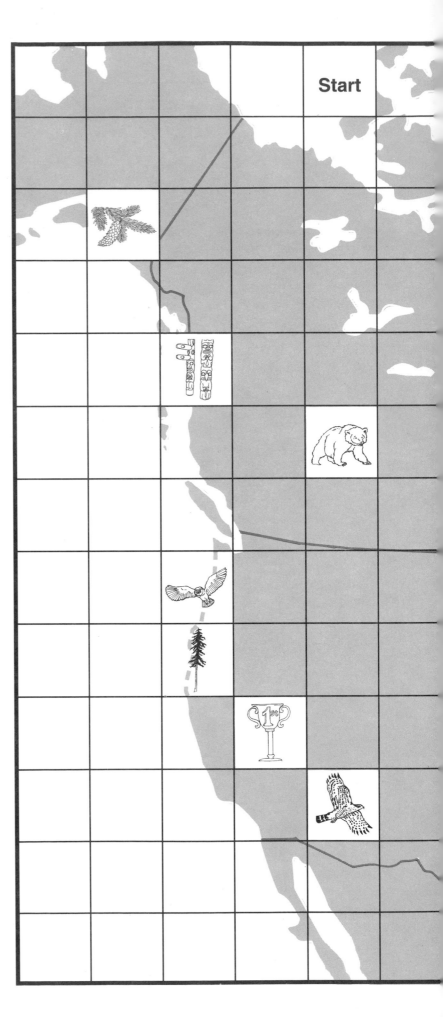

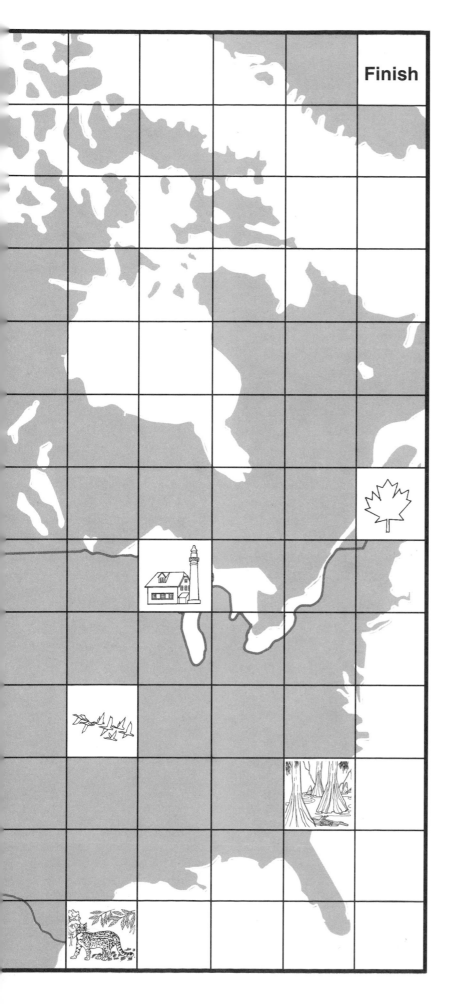

Finish

Forest Trek

Object:

Try to be the first player to visit all these ancient forests and reach FINISH.

You will need:

- A die (one of a pair of dice), or six objects marked 1 through 6.
- A playing piece, such as a pebble, for each player.
- Paper and pencil.

How to play:

Place your playing piece at START. Each player rolls the die and moves that number of spaces in turn. You may move up, down, or to the side, but not diagonally. You may change direction during your turn. If you land on a square occupied by another player's piece, send that piece back to START. If you land on an ancient forest square at the end of your turn, record its symbol on your score sheet.

Forests can be visited in any order. When you have visited every forest go to FINISH. You must roll the exact number to land on FINISH.

If you learn about other ancient forests, you might like to add them to your game.

Old-growth forests remain on the Apostle Islands in Lake Superior mainly because lighthouse reservations were protected from commercial logging. Rare Canadian yew grows well on islands that have not had deer. Deer eat the yew like candy.

Many trees in eastern Canada and the northeastern states are deciduous. They lose their leaves before winter. People travel to the forests to enjoy the fall colors. Few ancient forest patches remain.

The northern goshawk lives in the mixed forests of Arizona. It is one of several animals that depend on old-growth forests. Like the spotted owl, it reflects the health of its mountain-forest habitat.

An army base at Fort Leavenworth, Kansas, provides habitat for warblers and other forest birds. Large pecan forests on the base were not cut. These forests are resting and feeding stops for migratory birds.

The markings of an ocelot's coat help it to hide in the leafy shade of the sugarberry and ash forests of Texas. But there are not many such forests left. The ocelot is an endangered species.

Some forests in the southeast are also swamps. Although bald cypress likes to grow in standing water, its seeds sprout only after a severe drought. Water-loving animals like turtles share the swamp.

Tree Math

1243

A seedling sprouts.

1582

Fire! The tree survives.

1693

The tree dies. It is now a standing snag.

1776

Windstorm! The snag falls.

1854-59

Drought! Moisture in the log helps plants survive.

1993

The log is now part of the forest soil.

How long did the tree live?   _____

How many years did it spend as a standing snag?   _____

How long did it take to disappear once it fell?   _____

How long was it dead?   _____

How long was it around altogether?   _____

How can you tell the age of a living tree? A tree adds a new growth ring to its trunk each year. So you can tell the age of a tree by counting the growth rings. Dark rings are summer wood. Light rings are spring wood. One dark and one light ring is a year's growth. A tree corer provides a way of counting the rings without cutting down the tree.

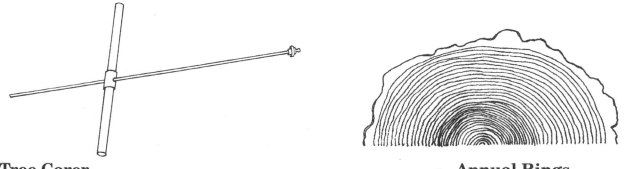

A Tree Corer

Annual Rings

The Science Team

People who study the relationships between living things and their environment are called ecologists. Forest ecologists are like detectives. They look for clues about the forest residents and figure out how the parts fit together. Sometimes other scientists help them. The types of scientists who help forest ecologists are listed below.

The letters in the name of the subject these scientists study are mixed up. **Sort them out and then draw a line to the equipment each scientist might need**.

A **zoologist** studies

_____
(salmian)

An **entomologist** studies

_____
(tesincs)

An **ornithologist** studies

_____
(dsrib)

A **geologist** studies

_____
(krcos)

A **botanist** studies

_____
(tpsnla)

A **mycologist** studies

_____
(ifnug)

binoculars

live mammal trap

microscope

net

hammer

plant press

Answers on last page

The upper layer of leaves and branches where the treetops meet is called the **canopy**. Getting to know who lives 200 feet up is not an easy job. Climbing a tall tree is a lot like climbing a mountain. It takes training, safe equipment, and a good head for heights.

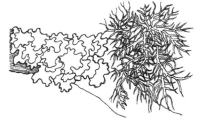

Here, a botanist is looking for **epiphytes**–plants that live in trees and get their water and nutrients from the air. Lichens are common epiphytes. Some of them don't just get a free home. They take nitrogen from the air and change it into a form to help feed the trees that support them.

Lichens grow slowly, but live for a long time. They can stand heat, cold, and drought, but they cannot stand air pollution. Where you find lichens, you know the air is clean.

Marbled Murrelet

If the botanist climbs high enough, she might find a marbled murrelet's nest. Until 1974, no one knew for sure where the murrelet nested. It is a seabird, but the female usually lays a single egg on a mossy branch in the canopy of an old-growth tree. The tree must be around 150 years old and mostly within 33 miles (55 km) of the coast. The parents take turns at fetching fish for their fledgling. With so many big trees being cut in the coastal forests, the murrelet has a hard time finding a nesting site. It is a **threatened** species. This means it is likely to become **endangered** in the near future. An endangered species is in immediate danger of extinction. If it becomes **extinct**, it is gone forever.

Trees-on-Stilts Mystery

Sheryl Holmes, the forest ecologist, had a mystery on her hands! Two facts about some very old hemlock trees puzzled her:

- The trees were growing in straight lines as if they had been planted. But who could have planted them hundreds of years ago?
- The roots were growing out of the trunks several feet above the soil. Why were those old hemlock trees standing on stilts?

After some deep thought, Sheryl had the answer to the first problem. No one planted the trees! When she sketched the chain of events that led to the trees growing in a straight line, she found that she had solved the trees-on-stilts mystery as well.

Sheryl's cards are mixed up. Can you put them back in the right order using her notes to help you?

Journal Entry:

I have just solved a mystery that goes back hundreds of years. Long ago a big tree crashed to the forest floor. Bark beetles flew in and invaded the log. They brought fungus spores with them. Threads of the fungus spread through the log making it rot.

Then hemlock seeds landed on the damp wood and sprouted. Slowly their roots grew around the log and down into the soil below. When the old log finally rotted away, it left a straight line of hemlock trees growing on stilt-like roots.

Sheryl Holmes

22

A-maz-ing Mushrooms

Mushrooms come in all sorts of colors, shapes, and sizes. They can look like dunce caps, shelves, or spheres.

Are mushrooms plants?

Scientists used to divide all living things into two groups or kingdoms: the plant kingdom and the animal kingdom. Plants make their own food. They contain a green pigment called chlorophyll, which lets them use the sun's energy to turn carbon dioxide from the air and water from the soil into sugars. Animals get their food by eating plants or other animals.

Mushrooms do not contain chlorophyll. Like animals, they get their food second-hand, so they are not plants. But they are not animals either. So scientists decided to put them in a new kingdom named **fungi**. Mushrooms are among thousands of different kinds of fungi. (One is called a **fungus**.) The mushroom is the fruiting stage. Most of the fungus consists of hidden threadlike **hyphae** under the ground or in rotting wood. Fungi are important members of the decomposition team, helping rot wood and other dead material. Over 500 kinds are found in the ancient forest.

Mushrooms are aboveground fruiting bodies.

Truffles are underground fruiting bodies.

Threads of a fungus are called **hyphae**. Hyphae comes from the Greek word for "web."

Spores

New fungi grow from **spores**. Spore comes from the Greek word for "seed."

Find your way to the mushroom through the tangled hyphae in the log.

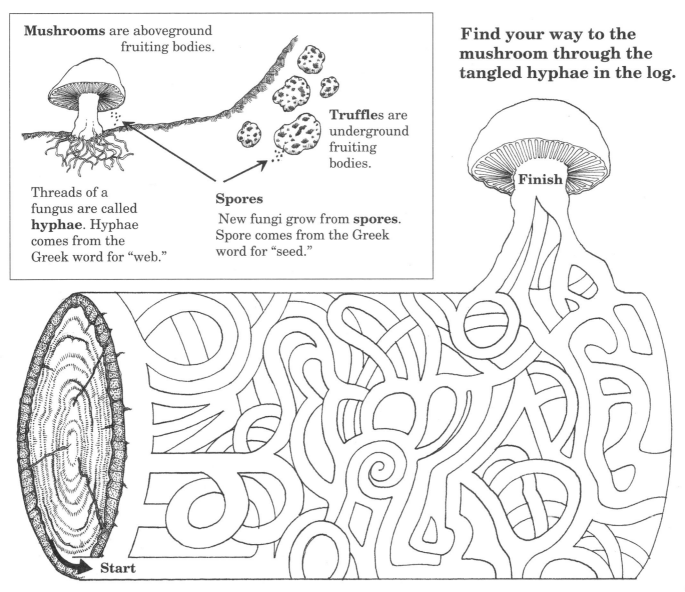

Finish

Start

Three-way Partners

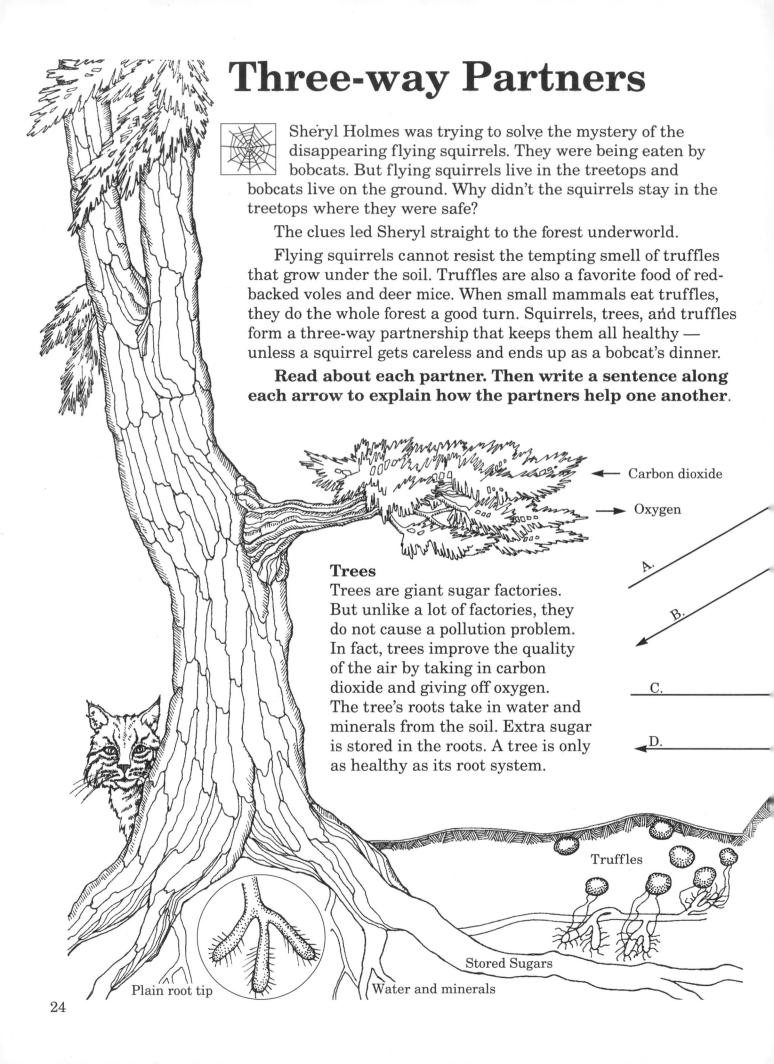

Sheryl Holmes was trying to solve the mystery of the disappearing flying squirrels. They were being eaten by bobcats. But flying squirrels live in the treetops and bobcats live on the ground. Why didn't the squirrels stay in the treetops where they were safe?

The clues led Sheryl straight to the forest underworld.

Flying squirrels cannot resist the tempting smell of truffles that grow under the soil. Truffles are also a favorite food of red-backed voles and deer mice. When small mammals eat truffles, they do the whole forest a good turn. Squirrels, trees, and truffles form a three-way partnership that keeps them all healthy — unless a squirrel gets careless and ends up as a bobcat's dinner.

Read about each partner. Then write a sentence along each arrow to explain how the partners help one another.

← Carbon dioxide

→ Oxygen

A.

B.

C.

D.

Trees

Trees are giant sugar factories. But unlike a lot of factories, they do not cause a pollution problem. In fact, trees improve the quality of the air by taking in carbon dioxide and giving off oxygen. The tree's roots take in water and minerals from the soil. Extra sugar is stored in the roots. A tree is only as healthy as its root system.

Truffles

Stored Sugars

Plain root tip

Water and minerals

24

Flying Squirrels

Flying squirrels don't really fly. They glide, supported by flaps of skin between their front and back legs. Some nest in old woodpeckers' holes or other cavities. Others make their own nests. One of their favorite foods is truffles. Truffles are rich in protein and water. Spores in the truffles pass through the squirrel's stomach and fall to the ground in its droppings. Under the right conditions, new fungi start to grow. Eventually the threads reach the tree roots.

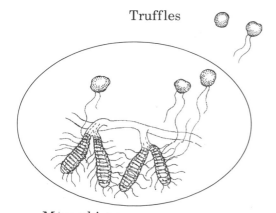

E.

F.

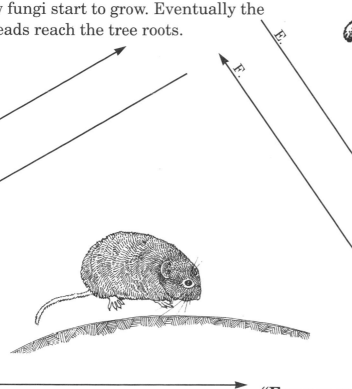

Truffles

Mycorrhizae:
root tips with fungal threads

"Fungus-roots"

Some fungi grow around or inside roots to form **mycorrhizae** (my-cor-RISE-zee). Mycorrhizae means "**fungus-roots**." These roots have more branches than plain roots do. They take up more water and minerals from the soil. The fungi help protect the roots from disease. Trees grow better when mycorrhizae are present. In return, the tree provides the fungus with sugars stored in its roots. The fungus produces underground truffles that contain spores. For these spores to reach new places, they must first be eaten by animals such as the red-backed vole or flying squirrel.

Answers on last page

Forests and the Ocean

Keeping Connecting Links Healthy

 The forest and the ocean belong to different ecosystems, but the health of one is related to that of the other. Water is one link between them. Clouds move in from the ocean. Rain finds its way into forest streams and back to the ocean. These streams are a link for animals as well as water.

Salmon spend time in both the streams and ocean. Young salmon, or **fry**, hatch from eggs buried in gravel in a streambed. As they grow, they migrate from the streams to the ocean. Those that don't end up as dinner for tuna, seals, dolphins, or people try to find their way back to their home stream to **spawn** or lay eggs. The adults then die and their decaying bodies return nutrients to the stream.

A salmon's journey is filled with danger. In many rivers they are totally gone. In others, they are threatened or endangered. Books such as *Discovering Salmon* tell of the many threats to these extraordinary fish. Follow the salmon story in the circles.

Different ecosystems such as the ocean, forest and stream are connected. Often we overlook the connections.

How many things are happening along the stream on the next page that might be harmful to salmon? Can you find some things that might be helpful?

Ideas on last page

Sun

Snow

Rain Cloud

Clouds Form

Lake

Water Evaporates

Salmon spend several years in the ocean before returning to their home

Ocean

Baby salmon hatch.

Females lay eggs in gravel of clear stream.

Fry spend several months or more feeding and growing.

Gravel covered by dirt in water.

Smolt undergo changes so they can live in salt water.

What other animal have you learned about that links the forest and the ocean? Draw its picture here and in the blank circle in the forest.

Fallen trees form another link between the forest and the ocean. Branches and twigs that wash down rivers add to the nutrients in the sea. Along the coast, huge logs and tangled roots help protect the shoreline. They make good perches for birds. Floating logs provide an anchor for shellfish and other sea creatures. Schools of fish often seek out their shade.

Forest Fire

Lightning has started a forest fire. Do forest or park managers call in fire fighters? Or should they let the fire burn itself out? It is often hard to decide. Putting a fire out is not always in the best interest of the forest. Fire is a natural force. It helps the forest renew itself. Even an ancient forest is always changing.

Fire can burn in the undergrowth without damaging the trees. Some plants and animals are adapted to fire. Trees like the coastal redwood have fire-resistant bark. Douglas-fir grows well following fire because it does not like to be shaded by other trees. Some seeds can only sprout after fire.

A long period without fire lets dead twigs, branches, and leaves build up on the forest floor. Shrubs grow tall. When a fire finally starts there is lots of fuel. The fire burns hot and fierce. Flames roar up the branches to the treetops causing a crown fire. The big trees die. The forest has to start over.

Match these plants and animals with how they have adapted to fire.

Answers on last page

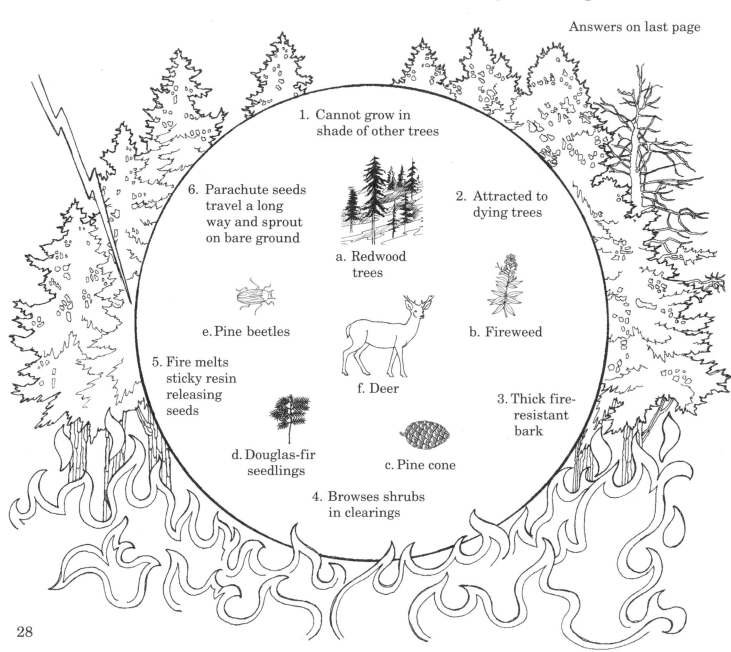

1. Cannot grow in shade of other trees

6. Parachute seeds travel a long way and sprout on bare ground

2. Attracted to dying trees

a. Redwood trees

e. Pine beetles

b. Fireweed

5. Fire melts sticky resin releasing seeds

f. Deer

3. Thick fire-resistant bark

d. Douglas-fir seedlings

c. Pine cone

4. Browses shrubs in clearings

Fragmented Forest

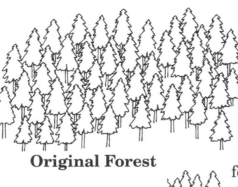

Original Forest

Today, forests are mostly cut down for lumber. Often all the trees in a forest are removed. This is called **clear-cutting**. The deep green forest covering the land is broken into small patches, farther and farther apart. When the remaining forest looks like patches or islands, scientists say the forest is **fragmented**.

Fragmented Forest

To play the game on the following pages, you become a young female or male owl. As a young owl, you need to leave home to find your own habitat. There is not enough room left in the forest where you hatched.

Object: Your owl must find a large enough habitat that is suitable to live in with a nesting site for laying eggs and raising young.

You will need:

- Two playing pieces –
  1. a small pebble or marker for the time line.
  2. a marker to follow the game path. Your marker could be a pebble or coin, or trace one of these owls. Decide if you are going to be a female or male. They look alike, but you may want to color them different colors for this game. Cut out the pattern, and tape a penny to the back. It is best to have an even number of males and females.
- Three objects (paper or pebbles) numbered 1, 2, and 3, in a container.

Female Owl    **Male Owl**

Directions:

1. Place your playing piece at START. Draw a number to see who goes first.
2. To find out which path your owl takes, draw a 1, 2, or 3. You will take that path.
3. To start your turn, draw a number and follow the instructions on the board. When you land on a junction, draw a number: 1 takes one path, 2 or 3 the other path.
4. After each turn, move your time marker along the time line. You hope to find new habitat before you run out of time
5. To occupy a nest site and FINISH, you must draw the exact number. For a male, no other owl may be in the area when you arrive. For females to stay, the area must already have a male owl. (You may ignore this rule if you are playing by yourself.)
6. When a male owl reaches FINISH first, he may "hoot" and call a female. If the female hears a male calling, she takes an extra turn without moving the time line marker.
7. Each owl that finds a suitable nesting site before time runs out is a winner.

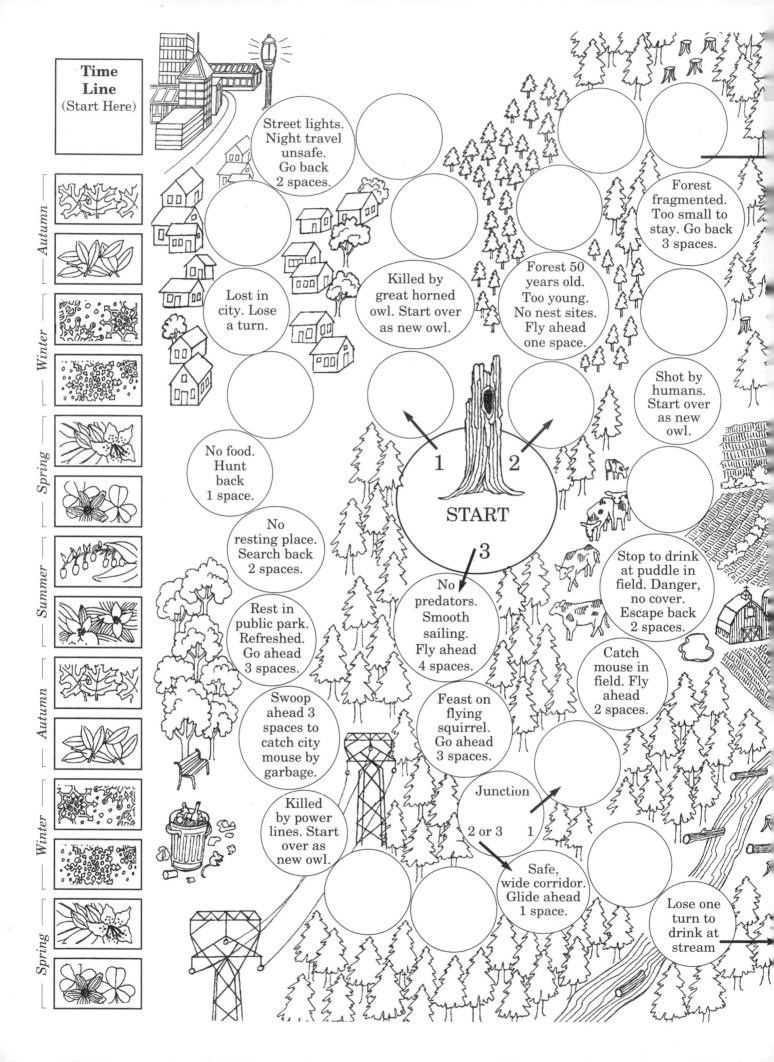

Time Line
(Start Here)

Autumn

Winter

Spring

Summer

Autumn

Winter

Spring

Street lights. Night travel unsafe. Go back 2 spaces.

Forest fragmented. Too small to stay. Go back 3 spaces.

Lost in city. Lose a turn.

Killed by great horned owl. Start over as new owl.

Forest 50 years old. Too young. No nest sites. Fly ahead one space.

Shot by humans. Start over as new owl.

No food. Hunt back 1 space.

START
1 2
3

Stop to drink at puddle in field. Danger, no cover. Escape back 2 spaces.

No resting place. Search back 2 spaces.

No predators. Smooth sailing. Fly ahead 4 spaces.

Catch mouse in field. Fly ahead 2 spaces.

Rest in public park. Refreshed. Go ahead 3 spaces.

Feast on flying squirrel. Go ahead 3 spaces.

Swoop ahead 3 spaces to catch city mouse by garbage.

Junction
2 or 3   1

Killed by power lines. Start over as new owl.

Safe, wide corridor. Glide ahead 1 space.

Lose one turn to drink at stream

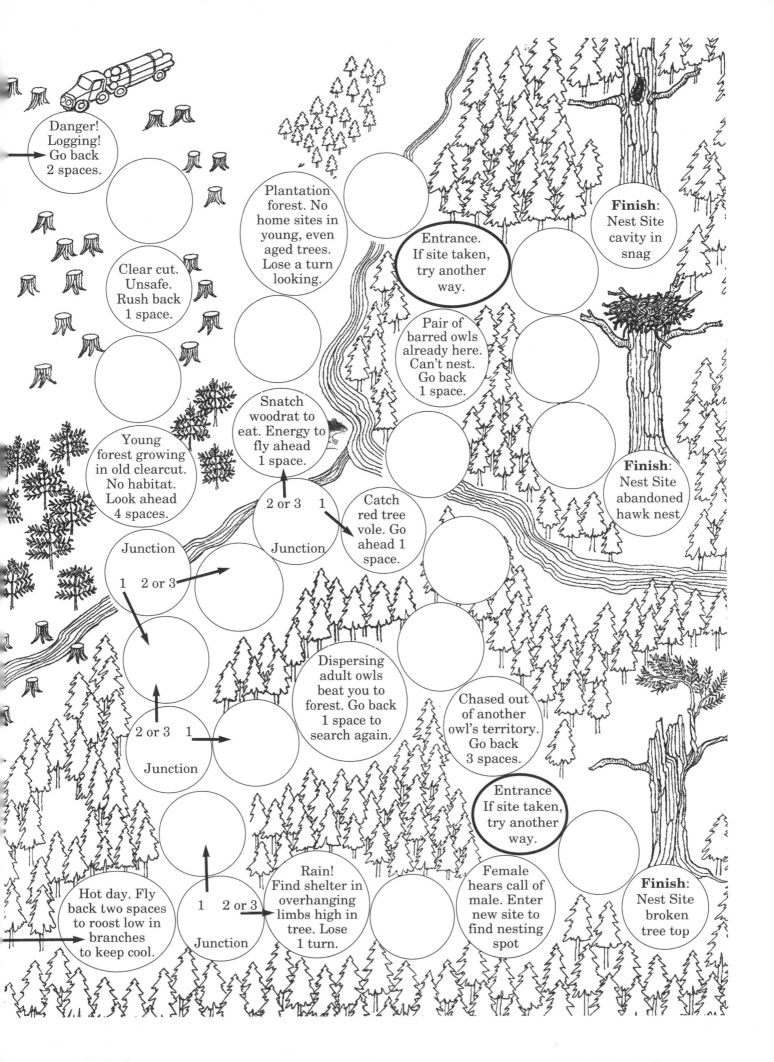

Danger! Logging! Go back 2 spaces.

Clear cut. Unsafe. Rush back 1 space.

Plantation forest. No home sites in young, even aged trees. Lose a turn looking.

Entrance. If site taken, try another way.

Finish: Nest Site cavity in snag

Pair of barred owls already here. Can't nest. Go back 1 space.

Young forest growing in old clearcut. No habitat. Look ahead 4 spaces.

Snatch woodrat to eat. Energy to fly ahead 1 space.

Finish: Nest Site abandoned hawk nest

Junction

2 or 3   1

Catch red tree vole. Go ahead 1 space.

1   2 or 3

Junction

Dispersing adult owls beat you to forest. Go back 1 space to search again.

Chased out of another owl's territory. Go back 3 spaces.

2 or 3   1

Junction

Entrance If site taken, try another way.

Hot day. Fly back two spaces to roost low in branches to keep cool.

1   2 or 3

Junction

Rain! Find shelter in overhanging limbs high in tree. Lose 1 turn.

Female hears call of male. Enter new site to find nesting spot

Finish: Nest Site broken tree top

Who is to Blame?

 It's not the people who cut the trees who are responsible for our disappearing forests. Everyone who uses wood is part of the problem. And that means all of us.

From early times to the present day, we have found uses for many of the kinds of trees that grow in North America. **Match the products on the two page with the trees below.**

_____ A. Telephone poles, structural timber

_____ B. Syrup

_____ C. Native American totem pole, diapers, clothing , bark basket

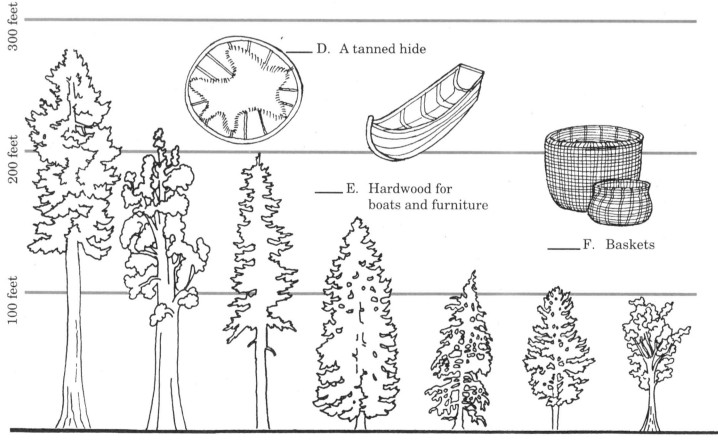

_____ D. A tanned hide

_____ E. Hardwood for boats and furniture

_____ F. Baskets

300 feet							
200 feet							
100 feet							

1	2	3	4	5	6	7
Redwood	**Sequoia**	**Douglas-fir**	**Sitka Spruce**	**Hemlock**	**White Pine**	**Cypress**
Resists rot in wet conditions	Soft and brittle, very little value	Straight trunks with even diameter	Strong, flexible wood	Tannin-rich bark used by Native Americans	Coastal trees with straight trunks	Wood lasts well under wet conditions

There is only so much wood to go around. To save the ancient forests, we need to reduce our demand for wood products. The paper for this book was once a living tree.

Answers on last page

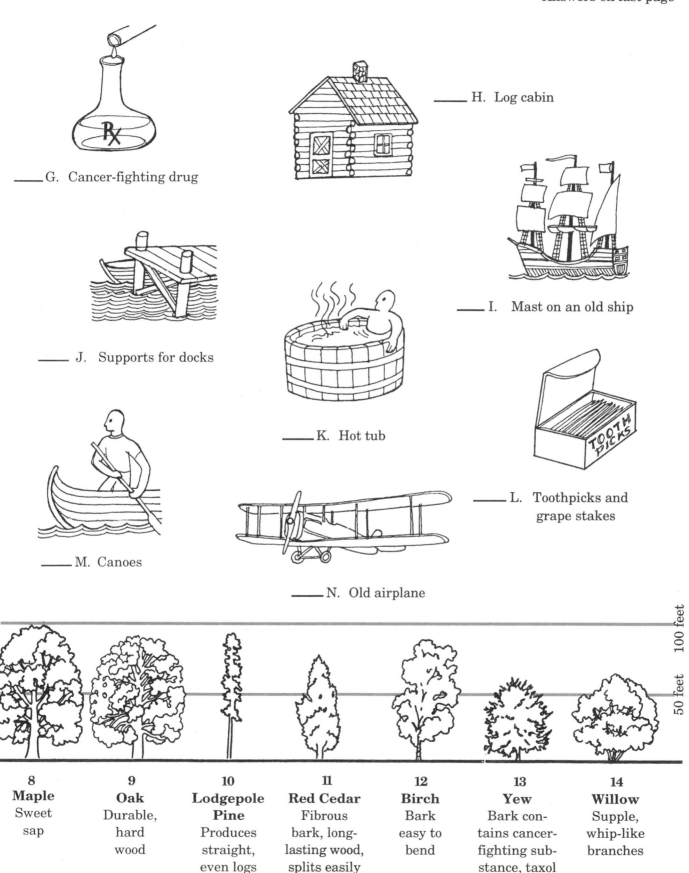

_____ G. Cancer-fighting drug

_____ H. Log cabin

_____ J. Supports for docks

_____ I. Mast on an old ship

_____ K. Hot tub

_____ L. Toothpicks and grape stakes

_____ M. Canoes

_____ N. Old airplane

8	9	10	11	12	13	14
Maple	**Oak**	**Lodgepole Pine**	**Red Cedar**	**Birch**	**Yew**	**Willow**
Sweet sap	Durable, hard wood	Produces straight, even logs	Fibrous bark, long-lasting wood, splits easily	Bark easy to bend	Bark contains cancer-fighting substance, taxol	Supple, whip-like branches

100 feet

50 feet

Plant More Trees?

Leave Some Behind

The Traditional Way

By planting fast growing trees and using fertilizers, we can grow more trees. Planted forests provide a lot more timber than natural forests do. To prepare the land for planting, the logged area is burned. This gets rid of unwanted wood and weeds. The new tree seedlings get all the food and sunlight. The trees grow straight and tall and are all the same age. However, a planted forest provides poor habitat for old-growth wildlife species. Disease and insect pests can spread quickly.

New Forestry

There are more forests now than in 1920. Many have grown back naturally. Others have been replanted. New forests are different from original forests. Some are managed so there is wood for people to use.

Foresters are exploring new ways of managing forests. Instead of clear cutting, loggers leave some dead snags, some living trees of different ages, and fallen logs. The new forest then has features of an old-growth forest. The soil is protected from washing away. Nutrients return to the soil. Habitat for wildlife is more varied.

What can we do?

Shape Poems

 People often show their love of nature by writing poems or drawing pictures. A shape poem is both a poem and a picture. Draw shapes and write your own poems about parts of the forest in the boxes below.

The snag stands like a finger pointing to the sky. It no longer lives, but it is full of life. Its branches are roosts. And holes are nests. Someday it will crash to the earth. But for now it is a standing snag.

Trail of Forest Words

Across:

1 & 6. The _____ owl and the tailed _____ live in the ancient forest.

7. Many plants grow on _____ logs.

9. The forest _____ includes living and nonliving parts.

10. Many animals use fallen _____ as highways.

11 & 13. Trees of many _____ and _____ grow in the ancient forest.

12. _____ helps the forest renew itself.

14. Ancient forests are also called _____ growth forests.

15. Logs in _____ change the course of a stream.

Down:

1. Standing dead trees are called _____ .

2. Flying squirrels love to eat _____ .

3. _____ of fallen trees is an impotant job of fungi and insects.

4. An animal's _____ is its home.

5. An _____ species is in danger of going extinct.

8. A forest _____ studies how living things interact with their environment.

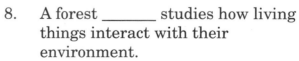

Answers

p. 6 and 7 Forest Neighborhoods: A. Snags: Standing dead trees B. Fallen logs on land C. Fallen logs in water D. Large old trees E. Trees of many ages and sizes

p. 9 High Density Housing: 1—Termite; 2—Wood-boring Beetle; 3—Carpenter Ant

p. 10 and 11 Apartments:

6	Bat	7	Pools
5	Bobcat	8	Shallow water
3	Hawk	11, 13, 14	Cover for fish
4	Woodpecker	10, 11, 12, 13	Bank
6	Brown creeper	11, 12, 13	Shade
1, 2	Spotted owl	9	Food source
2	Flying squirrel	8, 10	Air bubbles
4, 6	Beetle	14	Food for insects
6	Tree frog		

p. 19 Tree Math: The tree lived 450 years. It stood as a snag for 83 years. It took 217 years to disappear after it fell. It was dead 300 years. It was around 750 years altogether.

p. 20 The Science Team: Zoologist—animals—live animal trap; Entomologist—insects—net.; Ornithologist—birds—binoculars; Geologist—rocks—hammer; Botanist—plants—plant press; Mycologist—fungi—microscope. Actually, all the scientists might use most of the equipment at some time or another.

p. 22 Trees-on-Stilts Mystery: D, C, E, B, F, A

p. 24 Three-way Partners: A. Trees provide nesting and hiding places. B. Squirrels transport fungus spores helping trees grow. C. Trees provide fungus with food. D. Mycorrhizae help roots take in food and stay healthy. E. Squirrels spread fungal spores F. Truffles provide protein and water .

p. 26 Forests and the Ocean: Harmful things include roads and logging too close to streams; logging causes erosion, so salmon eggs are covered by dirt in water; with no trees, flooding is occurring along the left hand stream; A helpful thing is the people planting trees along the stream. The marbled murrelet goes in the blank circles.

p. 28 Forest Fire: 1–d, 2–e, 3–a, 4–g, 5–c, 6–b

p. 30 Who is to Blame? 1–K, 2–L, 3–A, 4–N, 5–D, 6–I, 7–J, 8–B, 9–E, 10–C, 11–C, 12–M, 13–G, 14–F

p. 39 Crossword

p. 20   Pattern for Forest Mobile

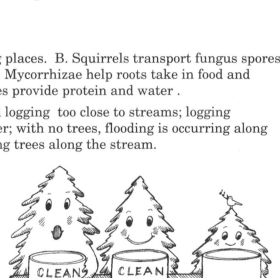

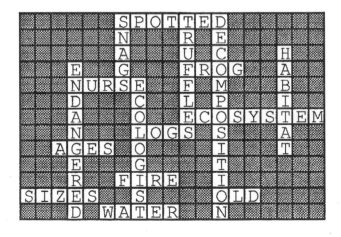

What services do forests provide?

Trees clean air by removing carbon dioxide, make oxygen which we breathe (6 tons of oxygen for one acre of forest), keep soil from washing or eroding away, protect rivers and streams keeping water clean, and provide beauty and recreation for humans. All these services are free!

40